I0183231

SORROW'S EGG

First published in 2011 by
The Dedalus Press
13 Moyclare Road
Baldoyle
Dublin 13
Ireland

www.dedaluspress.com

Editor: Pat Boran

Copyright © Katherine Duffy, 2011

ISBN 978 1 906614 40 9

All rights reserved.
No part of this publication may be reproduced in any form or by
any means without the prior permission of the publisher.

Dedalus Press titles are represented in the UK by
Central Books, 99 Wallis Road, London E9 5LN
and in North America by Syracuse University Press, Inc.,
621 Skytop Road, Suite 110, Syracuse, New York 13244.

Cover image © iStockphoto.com/Jamie Farrant

The Dedalus Press receives financial assistance from
The Arts Council / An Chomhairle Ealaíon

the arts council
funding
s chomhairle
literature
ealaíon
artscouncil.ie

SORROW'S EGG

Katherine Duffy

DEDALUS PRESS
DUBLIN, IRELAND

ACKNOWLEDGEMENTS

Acknowledgements are due to the editors of the following, in which a number of these poems, or versions of them, originally appeared: *The Irish Times, Poetry Ireland Review, The Shop, Orbis, Carapace* (South Africa), *De Brakke Hond* (Belgium), *Poetry Daily* (website), *Peterloo Poetry Competition Anthology 2005* and *Poetry Now Anthology 1999* (Dún Laoghaire-Rathdown County Council).

For my mother, Elizabeth Duffy

Contents

Sorrow's Egg

To a Cooking Apple at Twilight

On the brink of dark I have you in my hand—
a hard green vivid thing. I'd forgotten
how fast air tarnishes your flesh,

the arsenal of knives spoons rolling pins
it took to sugar and stew you into submission,
how sparing you are of your sweetness. Miser,

or bankrupt, everything gone
on frivolous blossom. Organic by default,
for who would bother

to shower you with gifts. Orphan,
shucked into wet grass by a feckless tree,
my grey-skies cold-wind hard-times bad-news apple.

With know-how I'd almost forgotten
I'll make comfort food of you. I'll tuck you
in buttery blankets. First, we pare a tell-tale curlicue.

Aria

An odd carolling wakes me,
keening from left field,
from somewhere else entirely.

Is it wind in the wires?
A banshee?
A child

with a clunky puzzle,
at last I match the sound
to you, your shoulders lapsing,

drowning in flowers. Your alveoli,
divas in the murky stadia of your lungs,
are singing their story—

a wild clear note
that darkens, spooling out
to eerie coloratura,

the music of damage,
now playing
in the arena of morning.

One Forward, Two Back

In the glaziers' quarter
at a crossroads, on a corner,
a shop of mirrors.

Twelve pretenders to yourself,
a school of startled glances
swims to a stop,

hangs in brackish light,
a rainy day, the air
rife with crescendoes.

See the green around your gills,
a crimson fleck in all of your eyes,
your silvered skin

alien yet recognised.
What happens next
is up to you:

like Alice,
step into the gallery
take a walk in hungry glass

and let the waters close
or whip around, set a course
for the cinema, bakery, bicycle-shop,

make a left for the realm of the hairdressers,
whistling a tune,
the street curling with you.

Haute Couture

On Howth Head
the sky is my big blue hat,
still bright around the rim
although the world begins
to dress down for evening.

An early moon's a jewel
in the navel of a muddy puddle.
Birds fly low, mocking a distant jet
with their easy unfuelled aeroplane chic.

Old's the new new, I'm told,
so my hat's the latest thing,
attached to my shoulders by tall,
avant-garde, invisible poles.

The promontory itself gives me height
more striking than any platform shoe.
I wobble slightly with the joy of walking here;
my hat quivers imperceptibly.

Travelling South

Traffic's long treacly grasp gives
and we go
plummeting down the map,
lovers in free fall
leaving the capital,

speeding past the bypassed towns,
whirling around roundabouts,
travelling south;
the road long known to us
though never the same
twice. At twilight

we steal under a river.
Bright daisies on the dash
say how far, how fast,
how close is emptiness;
the petrol station an ice-floe
slipping back as we sink

into a world of soft fields.
We could fall forever
down to a different dark.
Only the net of your memories
saves us: gaslight, Old Moore's
almanacs piled in the settle.

Going west at the end,
getting warm, getting old, roads
narrowing. Soon
we'll arrive,

drop the dusty cloak of the miles
on the back of a chair,
unpack another time.

Low Profile

Happiness wears an old coat,
acts like a character in a film,
identity yet to be revealed.
The plot winds on, a tale
of walks, drinks, talks. Only near the very end
does happiness step into the light.

By then the weather, everything's changed.
It dawns upon you who that is,
the down-at-heel gumshoe in a battered hat,
going about her business, shadowing
a gangly chef in chequered pants
who's slipped out the side door for a smoke
or the elderly couple with dog by the canal.

A cliché, but happiness won't be drawn
by margaritas, Mercedes, wedding dress,
but will skulk on a rainy day in a room
where someone's just gone back to bed
with a man or a book. Exits, sadly,
are a particular strength. Stage left
with eloquent footsteps.

Blood Sport

A breeze of fiddles—
he spins till he blurs
to a scrambled cypher.

The audience,
a raffish fringe around a Christmas cake,
emits a little crackle of applause.

On

through a labyrinth of loops and flips
the music urges him—
the world streams backwards from his fingertips.

He flees over solid cloud,
arching, flexing,
slowing to arabesque.

He crouches, unfurls,
flourishes,

falls.

The cameras are on him,
his ruined lip, his agonised
surprise, eyes
fearful as the numbers go up.

Place Your Bets Ladies and Gentlemen Please

Chips in a casino, the years
pile up, are cashed
or once more go
over the oblong possibilities.
Do you hear the croupier?
The wheel whirrs; the ball
leaps, dances, settles
on a number, a colour.

Red Shoe

Old wards, new wings,
corridors.
One foot in front of the other

brings me to my father.
How small he's grown—a changeling,
a dark thought

in his eyes, under the green.
His old smile
won't wear

but he likes my new red shoes,
notes that one has skinned my heel.
He deplores

the state of play,
the game on TV.
The tall lords come.

Not good, their words, *not
hopeful.* They shake their heads,
cannot foresee release,

not even for a season. Stay.
Swallow the black
seeds of pomegranate.

The afterwards of the car park,
fumbling at the lock,
the sun on my neck.

I put my foot down,
my raw foot, my red
shoe. I would go I would

drive to the end of the earth.

Crossing the Boyne

i.m. Peter Duffy, 1927—2004

This river boasts a battle
and two remarkable bridges.
One we crossed with you
by train, when we were small,
easily thrilled by your tall tales
of cotton wool foundations.

You and I drove over the other
a while ago, an autumn night,
its taut, bright stripes steepled over us.
I loved it for the joy it gave;
it drew your eye up,
took your mind off.

Inverted 'V'
of cable and lightwashed stone;
I'm still going over it.
Blue portal. Wishbone.
If I could make it fly apart,
I'd ask for one encore:

your voice singing its praises.

Crescent

The city, moon-shaped by the river's constant arm,
cracked houses, convoluted theories,
the lake not what I'd pictured from the song—

shallow and grey. Cars crawl on long
stilted bridges. A twist of beads on balconies,
the city, moon-shaped by the river's constant arm.

Best bib and tucker of bookshops, restaurants.
The ghost-tour leader spins slave-histories.
The lake is not what I'd gathered from the song.

In a voodoo temple: dolls, petitions, juju charms,
flotsam of heartfelt fripperies,
the city, moon-shaped by the river's constant arm.

Water and wind on cocktail lists. Candles burn.
Sludge, screams, dead dogs bulk out memories.
The lake is not as I heard it in the song.

Dredge up the light to rise above the harm.
Bones are dancing in three cemeteries.
The city, moon-shaped by the river's constant arm,
the lake not as I dreamed it from the song.

What We Bring

for my sister, Paula

We bring you flowers we know you loved:
stargazer lilies, yellow chrysanthemums,
roses when we're flush, roses

the jagged winds immediately set upon.
Are you under the cringing grass
or free above? Do the salt winds zoom

through, not costing you a shiver?
I have the pen you gave me when you learned.
When I use it are you watching at my shoulder?

Was what the fortune-teller told my cousin true?
Were they waiting for you on the other side,
your parents, sisters, friends, in party mood?

A robin hopped across my path today;
he stood his ground and looked at me so long
and hard—*piercingly.* I wondered.

Paula says you're with her in the car,
the car that was yours. Are we losing our minds?
We bring you flowers we know you loved

trying to stall you with colour and scent,
hoping to keep you tuned all hours
through veils of dark-blue atmosphere

to this reality show we call our lives.
We trim grass, wipe stone, arrange
in vases the pushy, persisting

flowers you loved. At your feet
we bank our questions; start with *where…?*
end with *when will the winds let up?*

The Empty Sky

How time races,
whips the water,
lunges towards beacon-glow,
flinches barely at a fence.

The card-game under the plum-tree
that balmy night is travelling,
getting away from me.
We won't find it

till Christmas,
won't know ourselves
in evening's telescope.
We are none of us

getting any younger,
none of us,
not since the sky was found
to be empty of reindeer.

The Real Thing

My father recommended
honey and lemon for colds,
make sure you leave the peel on;
remember, you can't beat
the real thing!

I'd roll my eyes
at the other end of the phone,
resolving to nip out
for Lemsip later.

Last night I took a knife,
sent tart wheels
into hot water,
spooned in amber streels

and stirred like a sorceror.
I raised my glass to the air,
to the generous, the lost,
the recipe's reciter.

Two Metaphors for Sorrow

Sorrow's a housewife
who sings as she shines.
She blows a wind clean through you,
makes glass of you,
good for shielding difficult plants,
for letting the sun in some other time.
She strips your gaze.
You'll see the comedy of machinery:
cement-mixers, steamrollers,
the sterling ugliness of a rusted gate.

Sorrow's a long street;
sometimes you'll wonder
if there's a vanishing point.

Letter of Reference

You have before you a loyal lieutenant
forever at the forefront of my retinue,
wearer of the most conspicuous liveries,
concocter of convoluted scenarios:
meltdowns, domino effects, apocalypse,
not to mention plain old falling flat on my face.

He rides shotgun; if ever I'm in danger
of feeling secure he'll spring into action,
flinging cold water, conjuring scenes
of loss, destruction, suffering. Failure,
success, it's all grist to him. A Trojan.
A twenty-four-seven grafter. Deliverer
of flawless performances. He achieves
objectives like there's no tomorrow
(which he's always maintained is the case anyway).

I didn't know he was thinking of quitting
or that you were thinking of taking him on.
He's been with me since birth, since the schoolyard.
I've grown accustomed to his histrionic face.
Would life be flat without his stratagems,
his powers of invention? I recommend him
highly, but feel it's only fair to inform—
I'm thinking seriously of offering him a raise.

Window

Light, splintered and sewn,
speaks impressionistically
of drowning and saving, of fishes
and water once walked upon.

Dark walls flank a roll-call—
cobalt, indigo, aquamarine
and the odd little green herring. Blue
flits in shoals across bright hats,

shoulders, faces, turning
to look at the future, a figure in the aisle
travelling slowly in fractured light.

Lost in the Kitchen

The piper's in the kitchen,
his arms full of music;
he works the bag, the bellows,
fretful reed, ominous drones.

He takes unruly air
under his wing,
sends it through complex plumbing.
Clear notes
pour from a rosewood chanter.

He raises his chin,
nods at a fly on the ceiling,
lifts a finger—

wars are lost,
old love
lost in the kitchen

and all that is not music
elbowed
out of the way of the tune.

Adage

It's love or the lack of it,
she said, wise hen,
when we turned up white-faced
to work in the factory.

Years of haunting the self-help shelves,
sifting for secrets;
it smoulders on. Love
or the lack of it. I'm trying it out

on all the big questions:
oil-greed, blood-lust, vertiginous shares.
If it holds I'll write a pamphlet,
maybe start a new religion.

Swans

I didn't know you'd followed me
the night I left the house

slammed, stormed

too drunk to drive
unable to get far enough away

pissed

You watched me walk to the canal
stand on the bridge

lingered

There were swans on the water
I was crying

wept

After a while I came back
hoping you'd ask for pardon

beg, implore

you wore a knowing smile
How were the swans? you asked

wryly, wrongfooting me,
transposing us to a minor key

where I could laugh again,
get off my high horse,
lay down my arms,

lay down.

The Old Ragbag of the Night

Insomnia, it's been a while
you're looking plump
the times that are in it
you must be cleaning up.

What'll you have—Ovaltine
chamomile, Barleycup?
We're almost friends; you may as well
sit down and take the weight off.

I see you're still toting it around
the old ragbag of the night
go on then—let its maw
fall open on the stroke of four.

I'm done with cotton wool.
Give me something I can work with:
swatches of scarlet
to flag my bright mistakes

cobalt for the chances missed
leopard splotch of ancient sins
velvet ache of unrequited lust
indigo

a deep abyss:
sickness, wreck, abandonment,
threaded with the lurex of the horrible.
Bring it on, if you must.

I'll tack, hem, blanket-stitch
appliqué upon the dark.
How busy I'll be kept
out of mischief, up all night.

Hark the Heralds

Once it was crisp
steps on stone
I listened for,

later the complaint,
the frame dragged over the step,
the articulate door.

Now it's a bloom of manoeuvre,
warm engine winding down,
the slowing, the stopping,

little birds, telling.

Shapeshifters

for Brian

Our younger selves
are out there somewhere, in the rain,
peering in, disparaging
the present us, the fat cats
we swore we'd never be,
warm and dry, drinking whiskey
by the fire in the hotel lobby.

Outside, drizzle is turned
by power of wind and sodium light
to a bas-relief of ghostly giants
crossing the middle distance,
hassled old gods
disappearing into the hills.

Don't we all, we say, sipping,
sell out in the end,
make for a luxurious *lios*
somewhere in out of the rain?

Later the wind dies;
the rain goes straight,
gives up its wild projections,
gets on with the business of falling.

Accident Blackspot

We were travelling fast,
leaving holiday behind,

when a milky fog boiled up
out of the fields of the midlands.

We'd been admiring
the trees, the sideways moon—

before that we'd been
bickering over some fact.

Fog swiped the moon,
a sickle behind its swirly back.

It drew a mystery down,
our beams turned broken and opaque.

All we had to go on
were hints, imperatives, a metaphor

springing out of the murky air, warnings
drifting under our wheels—a poetry

we could not afford to stop reading.

Pathetic Fallacy

I wake alone in my own half
of a bed in a house I own half of.
On the other side of curtains
chosen carefully, some time ago,
it's morning. The cat's clear
shadow plunges from the sill;
birds scatter up. The boiler wakes too,
hums a note as if about to sing,
then stops. It wants servicing,
expertise, whisperings.

Saving the Day

Strange thrift this
shortening one side
lengthening the other

fiddling with hems
evening up the edges.
With felt clicks

points shift, unseen
goalposts stray
and though the new

length is lovely
tiredness
inhabits me

clanking up and down
an ancient lift in a hotel
that has seen better days.

Amphora

Beneath this summer,
others lie—old cities
fallen, stratified in our hearts.
A rare and clever sun uncovers them,
whole frescoes: sea, sand, café-tables,
mountainsides, glimpsed—until drizzle
returns us to sifting for shards. We invent
a working model from a bird's thin bleat
from the mad-eyed geranium succeeding
in a corner of the yard. We dream
of warm, unbroken days,
reconstruct the season;
summer, a generous
amphora, an olive-jar
to store our fleshy memories in.

No Laughing, No Talking, No Moving

In stillness on their plinths, the living statues
brood on gesture. The crowd flickers
back and forth, lugging its weights and secrets.
When coins rain in his pail, pewter man
blunders from absence into dance.
The angel crafts a smile out of the dark.
An Egyptian wakes her beauty with a kiss.

No laughing no talking no moving!
a voice sang out once, homing
from the top of a long street to now,
to the smoker at the jeweller's door,
the florist deep in the crossword,
a young man crying into his phone,
white water of the crowd pouring around him.

Cinders in Carrowniskey

To Ceathrú an Uisce,
flooded quarter,
she goes, trying on
aloneness like a slipper,

wanting to sing with only the wind
for backing vocalist,
to be far from mothers and princes,
eat blackberries beyond Michaelmas.

Stepping lightly, she crosses
the gap-toothed bridge, the swan-flecked estuary.

Hermit

Your arm flows up, a surfer's wave,
the small light at the pinnacle
barely scratching this
abstract one you've chosen for a friend.
Your soles kiss sand or soil;
there are hills and other tests.

Your spine curved to your staff,
your hood implying mystery,
you flirt with the edges of boredom,
danger, cold. Sometimes it's good;
there are stars, a clean breeze,
the leaves alive with secrets.

You reach high ground, the world
a lit carpet below. Here's hoping
its patterns will give up their tricky ghosts.

Halt

We were like gypsies
burning the lichenous wood
of old apple-trees, gypsies
reeking of woodsmoke at evening,
and the fire, a luminous cuckoo
in the nest of the garden,
hissed appreciation
of each armful, green or dry,
swallowing even a wet mess
of fallen leaves, showering us
with small applause
that stole stitches, pierced cloth.

We sat on damp grass
by the side of our lives,
warming ourselves
at this easy image,
stretching our palms towards it.

Shanty

Windchimes translate
the whims of air.
Waves are pronouncing
their greens and their blues.

Lip-read through the double glaze
water and *sea* and *salt*
and *ocean* and *deep*
and *ocean* and *ocean.*

The tune will come to you.

Are We There Yet?

Where I go the moon goes
dragging her heels,
mouthing this is something she's been roped into,

her face bright but gnawed,
a Silvermint in a careless pocket,
her light lost in the lint of clouds.

If she'd look sharp this road could be
a ribbon
as it was for the highwayman.

She mocks—drawing from the deep
trees a white shape—a key piece;
she drops it, then there's just

me and the broken line,
beams swabbing the night,
me on my reluctant orbit,

her wish to be elsewhere
waxing on my shoulder,
burning in me, shining.

Overland

What rides by night
the road's lithe
spine, large brows
dark beneath lit tiaras?

What anxious beasts,
what friends endeavouring
to breathe, what carcasses,
toxic loads, secret fuels

are casketed, spirited,
dragged on eighteen-wheeled
giants, acting innocent,
like butter wouldn't melt?

Bubblewrapped

We are flirting with death-by-travel again,
closing our ears to what should be done,
looking away when the stewardess
makes her pantomime.

We have been to a sculptured city.
Its towers are packed in our hearts
and, in boxes, spoils of the market—
crystal, bubblewrapped.

Plusher cells accommodate
the skeleton's dance by the Town Hall clock,
the unpronounceable streets,
all the mulled wine we drank ...

Death lets us off, but the baggage is late;
we assume the various shapes of waiting,
annoyed to find this small torment
at the thin end of our adventure.

We're eyeing each other resentfully
when, with a shudder, the carousel starts
and we make away, hands full, hearts
blown and stretched as glass.

Fuchsia City

I've come here to be alone
but there's a city of insects in the fuchsia.
Flies are browsing in its dark boutiques,
moaning at the prices of the harlequin gowns.
Bees drink their brains out in showy emporia
then drone blues tunes 'bout how their queen
just don't appreciate them anymore.

In the leaves' multi-storeyed aerodromes
a tight schedule of arrivals and departures
operates—each second someone's taking off
or 'coptering down. I've come here for some peace
but those manic, stressed-out insects
keep whispering and muttering in my ear,

fretting they'll be late for the butterfly ballet,
bitten by the knowledge that paralysis, extermination,
is just a swat, an acrid spray away;
it's a risk no health insurance policy will cover.
I've come here to be idle but, unwittingly,
I've built a city of insects in the fuchsia.

On Encountering a Cockroach in Cyprus

My pride at getting on with spiders,
meeting mice without a bleat
comes to this fall. You
toddle towards me,
feelers waving,
my scalp ripples,
my flesh becomes a choppy sea.

Years of reading what the Buddha said,
how the Tao goes, have left their mark;
I cannot kill you
so I corral you
in the dank bathroom,
laying a towel under the door,
a blue towel but this is our green line.

All night a sinister
pottering on the other side.
Are you plotting to cross?
Mobilising more of your kind?
Obscene laughter at four o'clock
cracks the thin glaze of my sleep

and a flittered fact revisits me:
in the event of apocalypse
it's you who'll inherit the earth.

I observe the green line meticulously,
resort to the kitchen sink when I need to pee,
crossing only when the sun shows up.

There you are, small and skulking,
the colour of a blanched raisin,
paler than the richly evil shade I'd pictured.

When I look again you're gone.
I check my shoes,
rifle through my suitcase,
scuttle down the narrow stairs.

My taxi for the airport waits.
I step into silky, early air
trying to shake from my skin
prophecy's skittery patter.

Headroom

Under a slinky throw
of soot and cobweb, objects
doze, waiting for reprieve,
a phone call from the governor.

Things the wrong shade, things
chipped but not quite broken,
unwanted gifts, unstable candlesticks,
jigsaws missing the final piece.

I've come up with more
to add. In the gloom
house-truths reveal themselves:
the pitch of the roof, the way joists

run. I tiptoe around.
Shadows rehearse their roles:
haunted rocking horse, abandoned child,
an elephant, a worsening picture.

Softly I go, softly,
keeping myself to myself.

Rubicon

Picturing an important stretch,
I look it up on the internet
to find it was just a narrow stream.

Rickety bridge for an upstart general
choking on life in the provinces,
spoiling for a fight.

He crosses velvet syllables
but what brings me here, shadowing,
following close, holding the rail?

We set foot. The light is interesting,
the grass not greener nor less green.
The trees have a bluish hue.

You'd think the general, of all people, would march on
but like myself he's dilly-dallying,
looking behind him, trying to fathom

this river with jewels and faces in its name.

After the Tone

It's all she has of him,
his voice homing in
on a crackle of static,
things said granted
safe passage to deeper parts.
That's it for now,
a handset pressed
to the whorls of her ear—
inland child, listening.

Retreat

Me and my shadow
on a cold strand;
marram grass curves low
over the soft, undone sand.

A preacher rock
berates a stony congregation
while a long mean wind
works the strand, pushing waves
till they fall, blubbering.

From among my ribs
my shadow stepped,
took my arm, announcing
a wish to stretch its legs.

Gulls in a low-slung sky
swerve and warn.
The first drops. I'm glad as if
I'd danced for them—
excuse to turn,
get back to my shell.

I slam in,
invoke the radio,
the heater's wheezy forgiveness
tough love of the safety belt.

At the window a shadow
presses, panicking,
whisked into rearview, minimised,
waving, waving.

Silk Burns

The teacher reiterates:
this is a martial art.
The Eight Pieces of Brocade
was devised by a general, used to train soldiers.
Over the years it's been mistranslated.
It should read *'pull tendons till they break'*
and White Crane Flaps its Wings
really means *'rip shoulders under arse'.*

So those of us want to be
Waving Hands in Clouds,
Gazing Back at the Moon,
Picking Up Needles from the Ocean Floor,
Swimming like a Dragon
will have to take a rain check.

Words and meaning
are disenchanted lovers
warding each other off.
The teacher scolds. Silk burns
hissing through my hands.

Strange Grass

for Roger Doyle

Before us a sea of tall grass.
The real sea hides around the corner,
hunched and muttering a plot.

We shrug off the doors that don't lock,
a tap that won't turn, take to the terrace
resign ourselves to prairie.

Knife-leaves make vintage fabric of the sky.
The grass is not whispering;
silently it leans and strains.

The evening lacks a soundtrack.
We wish you could oblige.
The light is beautiful but not a truth-teller.

Burn the ocean's garbled song.
Slant down a cool steel rain. Rustle up
sounds for this tall, strange grass.

Endangered

silence on the eyes
compost for the flowering of dreams
hard to find unpasteurised

musky and smooth
rich and dizzying
it takes snuffling out

in paintings a line
a nugget a shrug
of hills a smear of poplars

stay in the light
play in the sun
childhood advice smoulders

a black field
where footfalls grow
people have been

erased here,
lovers and torturers
harboured equally

dark
defines and undoes
the known

an animal at the window
forceful and shy
showing up with an orb

a winking entourage
or alone
dressed as itself.

Reportage

Here is a tenderness
is not in our repertoire.
You and your brothers lift your uncle up.
The box is bathed in air.

You're my reporter at the front;
from you I hear how heavy it weighs
and how a man the wrong height
can cause a week of neck pain.

The undertaker walks backwards
before the different creature that you make,
coaxing you once around the old church,
dispensing with the traditional

three circuits, in deference to modernity
and treacherous ground. You say
you were in danger of stumbling,
dissolving into laughter.

Familiar hands have dug the plot,
older bones gently stowed
aside, then returned, tucked in
behind the clean new coffin.

You've buried the man who once described
laying his own last uncle down,
how the thought struck as they took their whiskey.
That's it! We're next in the firing line.

Creagh graveyard, Skibbereen, Co. Cork

Visitors

The house forbidden,
we took to the gardens;
we walked a Tarot landscape,
trees, tall and dark by a lake.

I spoke of a dilemma,
you of a new contentment
while the wind played
the hand it was dealt by the trees.

While we were talking
a cold-eyed trickster
had stolen out of the woods.
You welcomed him, said everything

was happening as it should;
now worms would comb the soil,
goblins dance,
and, in northern latitudes,

we would bask in firelight.
Still shuffling futures,
we crossed a narrow bridge.
Two swans veered away.

From the stone steps
of a turreted folly, we looked down
on a private burial ground
named, oddly,

Tír na nÓg.
The pool at its centre was dry,
stopped with a coppery swirl
of leaves, brittle memories of fish,

ornamental carp,
live and elaborate
as our own concerns, slipping
through the shallow dark.

Mount Stewart House, Co. Down

Sorrow's Egg

One magpie—
where is the sorrow?
New green on the trees,
blackbird with a loud beak.

Tawny robin
hops towards a crumb.
A pigeon with solid shoulders,
a civil servant of a pigeon,
returns to a beloved tree,
to a man with a pocketful.

The sky flexing its muscles,
the fountain beginning to fizz;
trees are taking
classes in shade.

Somewhere in all of this
sorrow's egg is
tucked away. Somewhere,
warming.

Infringement

Le gach bó a lao agus le gach leabhar
a mhacasamhail *

She doesn't spare him a thought,
covetous monk in the narrow weather
of an island prison. The breakfast table
a seared veldt, her daughter's glance,
withering, preoccupies her.

She presses paper to glass;
words flow from a dazzling shuttle.
Pages fall to her, children from school,
neatly tattooed, warm as bread.
She shuffles, collates, aligns.

He waits in a crowded alcove
where stories from childhood loiter,
hoping for another hour onstage—
a daredevil, scratching at vellum.

She straightens from stacking fresh paper
to find, on peripheral vision,
a soft print, hint of a cowl.

It comes back to her: cows, calves,
books, open and closed.
The whisper of a long cold sentence.

Closure

Time to put it away, that old coverlet,
in the linen-cupboard of your mind.
Before you fold it, you know you'll shake it out
one last time—you won't be able to resist
its chameleon cloth: flowing paisley,
houndstooth growling.

Over the years it's got everything on it:
coffee, cigarette-burns, body fluids.
An edge is torn, the centre worn thin,
but overall it's served you well.
You've done all you can with it. Time to abjure
the discreet dryclean, the invisible mend.

Put it away. The lavender you dried
from the garden where we sat—
throw a handful of that on it.

Twelve

Time in clean squares
hangs
from Bashō's, Issa's words.

Twelve moons,
parchment discs, whole or sliced,
a cool sequence

crossed by silhouettes:
frog, heron, crow,
a branch that behaves like a dragon.

Every day's twelve months
from another, an anniversary,
wooden or golden.

My calendar,
thin shield between
me and the sore old year.

NOTES

'Infringement', p. 66

'To every cow its calf and to every book its copy' was the judge-
ment handed down by High King Diarmuid Mac Cearbhail
against St. Colmcille in the first known case of breach of copyright.
Colmcille had copied illegally an important psalter belonging to St.
Finian. A battle ensued in which 3,000 died. As penance,
Colmcille went into exile on the remote Scottish island of Iona.

Dedalus Press
Poetry from Ireland and the world

Established in 1985, the Dedalus Press is one of Ireland's best-known literary imprints, dedicated to new Irish poetry and to poetry from around the world in English translation.

For further information on Dedalus Press titles, as well as audio samples and podcasts in our Audio Room, please visit **www.dedaluspress.com**.

"One of the most outward looking poetry presses in Ireland and the UK"
—UNESCO.org

www.ingramcontent.com/pod-product-compliance
Lightning Source LLC
LaVergne TN
LVHW011429080426
835512LV00005B/351